These Are My Senses

What Can I Hear?

Joanna Issa

Heinemann
LIBRARY

Chicago, Illinois

© 2015 Heinemann Library
an imprint of Capstone Global Library, LLC
Chicago, Illinois

Edited by Siân Smith
Designed by Richard Parker and Peggie Carley
Picture research by Tracy Cummins
Production by Victoria Fitzgerald
Originated by Capstone Global Library Ltd

Library of Congress Cataloging-in-Publication Data
Cataloging-in-publication information is on file with the Library of Congress.
ISBN 978-1-4846-0433-5 (paperback)
ISBN 978-1-4846-0446-5 (eBook PDF)

Image Credits
Alamy: Francois Werli, 7, Tetra Images, 17; Dreamstime: Carlosphotos, 8, 21 (left); Getty Images: Geri Lavrov, cover, lend Images - JGI/Jamie Grill, 10, Yang Liu, 9; Shutterstock: aceshot1, 12, Borislav Borisov, 6, 21 (right), 22 (right), back cover, Damien Richard, 14, Digital Storm, 4, 22 (left), jctabb, 16, 20 (right), Kalmatsuy Tatyana, 15, Lisajsh, 13, marco mayer, 5, Martin Novak, 19, Olly, 11, Sergey Lavrentev, 18, 20 (left)

Every effort has been made to contact copyright holders of material reproduced in this book. Any omissions will be rectified in subsequent printings if notice is given to the publisher.

Contents

What Can I Hear?

I hear a **loud** siren.

I have to cover my ears.

I hear a **quiet** sound.

A bird is quiet.

I hear fireworks.

I have to cover my ears.

I hear a quiet sound.

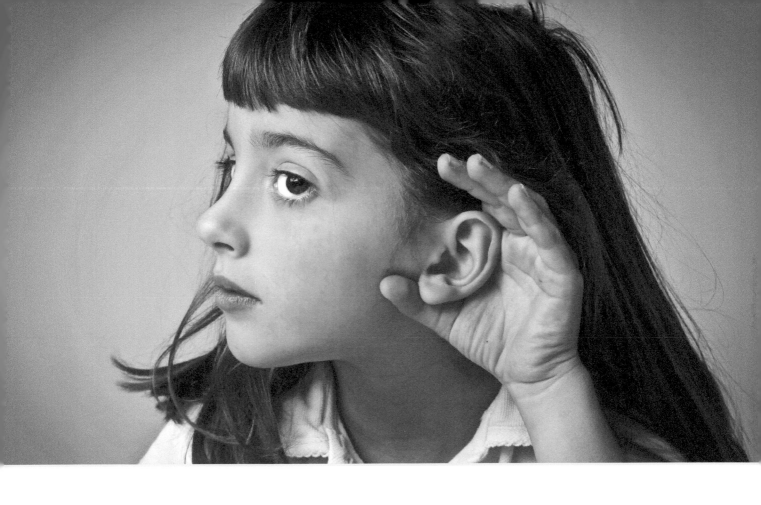

Rain is quiet.

I hear a drum.

I have to cover my ears.

I hear a quiet sound.

A cat is quiet.

I hear thunder.

I have to cover my ears.

I hear a quiet sound.

A whisper is quiet.

Quiz: Spot the Difference

Can you find the loud sounds?

The thunder and the fireworks are loud.
The whisper and the bird are quiet.

Picture Glossary

 **loud**

 **quiet**

Index